ETHIOP

ISHMAEL FIIFI ANNOBIL was born in 1958, in Ghana, where he started an early career in poetry and journalism. He has lived in the Sudan and Kenya, where he worked as a reporter and compiled his poetry, culminating in his acclaimed recital, *Criers on The Thresholds of Reality* (Nairobi 1983). He came to England as a correspondent, in late 1983. Inspired by a radio broadcast on Welsh poetry, he moved with his family to Wales, where he lived for eleven years, founding the international poetry festival, *Festival Iolo* (formerly *Iolo's Children*), and the cutting edge arts newspaper, *Circa21*. He is the founder of online arts journal *Chiaroscuro Magazine*, and of the international film collective, *Stonedog Productions* (London). His films include *In The Presence of Awe - The Transvangarde* (art documentary), *Kenji Yoshida - Artist of the Soul* (art documentary), *Salamander Walks* (a surreal feature), and *Hornsleth: Product of Love*, a documentary about controversial Danish artist Kristian Von Hornsleth. He has published two books of poetry (*Seven Horn Elegy* and *Ethiop*), and one music album, *Zingliwu*. His forthcoming books include *Portrait of a Man in Pain* (novel), *Inklings of Clay* (historical novella) and *Utopia of the Worms* (poetry). A master photographer, his images have been published in various publications, including *The Independent Newspaper*, and prestigious French magazine *M3*. Ishmael attended Christian Methodist Secondary School (Acrra, Ghana), studied Social Anthropology extramurally at Goldsmith's College, and undertook a PgDip in Visual Communications at West Herts College. He lives in London with his wife, Helen, and their two children, Brendan and Nana Yaa.

ETHIOP

ISHMAEL FIIFI ANNOBIL

totem

2nd Edition
Published in Great Britain 2017 by Totem
60 Swinley House, Redhill Street, Regents Park
London NW1 4BB

© Ishmael Fiifi Annobil 2017

All rights reserved under British and International
Copyright Conventions.

Subject: Poetry Title: Ethiop Author's Nationality: Ghanaian

ISBN 978-1-899151-06-6

Acknowledgements:
Sudan, Abalaa and The Stolen Sentence
were first published in Hydra (2000)

Cover illustration: *Away From the Slaughter*, by Ishmael Fiifi Annobil
Ethiop Illustartion: *Kaa Bi Olanmor Sane Ni Eye Bo Seke*, (*Do Not Question Your Umbilical Cord or be Maddened By It*), from *Abetei* by Ishmael Fiifi Annobil
Author's portrait by Nana Yaa Annobil

Designed and Typeset by Ishmael Fiifi Annobil

CONTENTS

6	Author's Note
9	The Welcome
11	Ethiop
13	The Earth We Lost
14	Sudan
16	Abalaa
17	Aqua Green
18	The Stolen Sentence
19	Flower Water
20	The Di-Hiraeth
23	Phoenix Is Back In Town
24	The Street dancer
26	Moondress
28	Yesu, Yesu
30	The Beseecher
32	Teardrop-Aqua Lumina
34	Vignettes
35	Shola The Unknown
38	Accordion Boy
40	The Last Drunkard
42	The Inglorious Dying
44	Stone
45	Pastorale
46	The Day Before
48	Family Home
49	Yet
50	The Mysterious Song of a Modern Kurd
51	Armah
52	Cicatrix

Author's Note

The poems *Ethiop*, *Shola the Unknown*, and *Abalaa* belong to the Diaspora Africans, whose sacrifices and great inventions were, and are, pivotal in the making of the West, despite the primordial wickedness against them. In acknowledging them, I also pay homage to the Maroons and Haitians, who took a stand and won; the valiant members of the Underground Railroad; the fine nation of Canada; those selfless Native Americans; and all others, who helped the overburdened African escape *that* American night.

Special thanks are due my parents for teaching me momentum; also to Judy (Chili) Hawes for her warmth, quiet encouragement and compassion; John Polka Allen for his altruistic energy and refined leadership; Deborah Snyder for understanding the space above people's heads; Kathelin Gray for having the heart of a harp; Susie Gault for restoring humour to intellect; Suzy Sureck for journeys poetical; and my in-laws, Maurice and Mary Jackson, for their spiritual nearness.

i.f.a

To Helen,

with whom I will always laugh

The Welcome

This is the land you deserted -
It's richer now, richer than the one
You are retreating from.

You have wandered, Ishmael; we couldn't
Keep the welcome any longer.
You have wandered the skies
In search of the black rainbow;
And we have roamed your many footsteps
For your scent.

Your ancestry has succumbed
To your absence, and to
The children you did not care to leave us.

We have withered in the Harmattan
Without your tears;
Winnowed like husks of January corn,
Tormented by our futile wish of death.

We singed our faces in the sun
For we aimed to side-step the sun to find God.

Animals in their pens hooted
After your shadow, trusting, as we were,
In their dredging sight. They failed.

But we have lasted-
We have broken the ice with pain:
Pain will abate when we seek our children
From the sky;
And we shall abide it when it seeks
To test our faith.

You are back, Ishmael;
You bear but the ordinary wisdom

Of bread and butter — the transcendence
Of pessimists.
We remember your face, for we gave it to you.
We recognize your old scars, for we nursed them.
Your mind we still see in the smile
We coaxed from you at birth.

Your words, however, we have chosen
To sacrifice,
For they walk a parallel path from ours –
Though they crave to echo the oracles, as ours do,
They arch like a camel's back.

We shall wash your dusty feet
And lay a mat for you to rest on.
      And tonight,
We shall lash your back with bitter herbs*
To cut into your veins the past you deserted.

You will rise at dawn to forgive yourself.

You will reach for our feet
And we shall place them at your lips.

You will rise at dawn.

(17 /8/98 Grangetown, Cardiff, Wales)

NB: The name of the protagonist is purely coincidental, and is used here to echo the Biblical Ishmael - Wanderer. The poem explores a hypothetical (if mythic) return to one's roots.

*Bitter herbs form a major part of the sacramental feast of the Homowo festival of the Ga of Ghana. Homowo is a major vestige of their Hebraic heritage, and it mirrors The Passover in every way, except a 'Twin Cult' detail, which follows a unique Ga cosmology.

to the Memory of Bob Marley

ETHIOP

Ethiop, you are a mountain.
Come rain or shine, you are a mountain,
Acute like love;
Yet precipitous like love itself.

You haunt your foe's mind's eye
With a bronze expression;
Playing on your verdigris of age
With a privileged smile —
You inspire fury in his vulgar heart.

He's come often to your slumber to seek
Your splay, like a prodigal
Sparked by a presumed welcome; (he is perverse!)

But he fails even to arc well into
That illusion, and capture its eye in his blood —
You have made him paranoid, you have.

Ethiop, your face makes him weary,
It shines of mercury,
Relief-ed like a water mask —
You are irksome, Ethiop.

You have called your foe to your feast:
With Socratic irony,
You have let him drink you under the table, then
He has burped into your eyes and called you humble.
You have laughed that privileged smile of yours.
You are mischievous, Ethiop.

He has shown his hand too soon - he knows now.
He doubts his own wisdom now - he is confused.

So he woos you with a pain-smile,
A furrowed forehead, – the depth of deceit –
A prayerful clasp of fingers, like kissing lampreys,
And wine shuddered with hemlock.
His narrowed heart
Whimpers at your feet with lurid passion:
He will kiss your corpse with shut eyes, for insane
transference, should you fall.

But you will keep standing tall, Ethiop,
For you are transcendent.

He will hate you forever.
And you, son of love, will love him forever.

For you are.

(5/10/98 Regents Park, London)

for Abigail Alling

THE EARTH WE LOST

Here lies the green plot–
It awaits your spade.

It has been replenished
By the careful arrogance of death.

If zestful, you might unearth faith
From its bowels;

Faith of nonplussed saints
Sent in vain to wash your eyes.

It lies under your kingdom
Like a prayer mat:

Neo-baptismal like first love,
almost.

(12/6/99 Regents Park, London, 3.15 am)

for John Allen

Sudan

We have all been crippled before
By your love of pain.

   You are the prosecutor of the trial.

We seek your breasts from rocks,
Like mythical milk founts, to
Undo the penury of your future.

We slap hands with your two Niles
Like old friends, to compare torture marks,
And to seize your faith with us.

   But such strength of hand! you
   Defy us like a grieving elephant.

We imagine shoals in your water,
     Every drop of it
That you boil deep into the night
To tantalise our hopes

— pot of rocks.

Do you ever stop and wash the dust off
Your children's faces, to see their beauty?
You wean your children too soon, Sudan.

Sages tell me you are a dormant censure,
Merely dredging our sick minds for the fuel
To announce your glory.

   But such revolutions I have seen

And
Hated.

Beware, they don't deliver the innocent!

      They merely wash the land
      In virgins' blood, and anoint thieves.

Didn't you once say you had the heart
Of an elephant, vigorous but pure in rage?

Haven't you once played host to lost strangers,
And broken your only crumb with them? —
      Are you not the great paradox?

We won't pray anymore, Sudan; it's all done.

We shall just sit here and wait for you:

      (Pessimists may pray at a desecrated altar;
      not us).

All your dust roads must lead to us,
Your children.

Remember.

(20/6/99 Regents Park, London, 12-55 am)

for Christine Handte

ABALAA

Where are the men of the first aplodo*
whose ambition for the blue yonder
transpired in this village and
held us captive for six long months

      Where did the albatross lead them,
      thirsty as they might have been
      for the trickle of nature,
      forlorn and homesick
      even as they harried their oars
      over the emblems of hope that
      dressed the sides of their canoe,
      whose resolute prow held live chickens
      for the gods of the sea
      and snorted through each wave
      like a whaler's retriever?

We are waiting on these shores for news,
tortured by sailors' tales of a phantom canoe
roaming the seas with its crew of begging ghosts.
But none mentions the chickens,
so we wait for news
of their new nation.

(2/2/2000 Euston -Watford, Silverlink train)

---

*Aplodo: a traditional sea quest amongst the Ga fishermen of Ghana, which has for centuries taken them to foreign lands, including the Americas, where some settle and never come back home. This author believes this to be one of the ways many Africans reached other lands, and became mistaken, purposely, by modern historians for slaves.

for Nana Yaa (formerly Vanessa)

AQUA GREEN

I dream a green river:
Not of moss
But the liquid scent of joy.

In its smile I'll baste
My passion
Before my surprise of sin.

To that very smile
I shall return to atone for
My lust, then learn love

Again, like a cinderling*
Does at the bellows
Of forgetful, forgiving rage.

I dream a green river
Whose lips elephants shall kiss
And hummingbirds
May cleave their flutes in.

(12/6/99 Regents Park, London 3am)

---

*Cinderling: a neologism from cinder; used here to symbolise naive, reckless youth. The purpose of this piece is to illustrate the stumbling efforts of modern industrialists to wake to the whimpers of the environment.

a note to the fascists of The Balkans and Africa

THE STOLEN SENTENCE

They lie fallow
In each other's cuddle,
Like octopuses
Distracted by light.

All the songs have withered.

Morning, the raw dissector,
Has greeted their stained
Curves,
Countering their dying consciences.

They've outlived
The illicit temper of night;

Reality will
Outplay them at this game.

(28/6/99 Regents Park, London)

for victims of drought

FLOWER WATER
(or rain dance)

This eye of earth
where
horses learned to kneel,

– they say rivers are God's nourishing tears –

if I see your teardrop again,
I shall
elope with it
to shame the sun-god.

(26/6/99 Regents Park, London)

dedicated to Ghana and Wales

THE DI-HIRAETH
(*a poem for two voices*)

I shall redeem my love from these ashes

        (though it lies on its side).

    I, lotus eater,
    Have roamed the other desert
    In search of free crabs
    But found cacti instead,
    Entwined; even they, by love.

Now I rise again,
Fired by the nectar of ascending memories (melanin),
To fly from such pain

        (though I am fond of bridges).

    Pruned by the wind of ice,
    I slither through the passage
    Of birth, into the impinging stirring,
    Almost pre-dating fire;

        (though I love eyes and flesh).

So that this my second journey (safari ya pili)*
May collapse time and free me, the lotus eater,
From face or voice,
And lapse my lament, with libidinal swiftness,
Onto a piquant sea that laps my two spheres.

I shall redeem my love from these ashes

        (though it lies on its side).

And if it wills,
This love may rise with me.
I am hastening time towards
Dream-gourds in flight.
I am elated by the fever.

Wind
Embraces my shoulders,
Like it would an avian,
Whispering
The journeyman's password:
"I love. I love. I love. I love".

Or is melanin, after all, like the sting of peyote
Behind the tongue of the initiate?
Or is melanin free like the whim of a cougar
At night?

What will I do with the trophies I find?
Which love came first? Which spice will I sniff first?

   Who am I? Who am I? Who am I?

(O, what plaintive hallelujah awaits this supplicant !?)

I am not the falsehood painted by spite

   (for your eyes only).

   I am the truth that
   Tempers wickedness.
   I am the seed swept against the gravel wall,

   (though the wind carries my song)

   I am the palm tree dispersing
   Invisible seed to flower your sinews.

I am melanin
I am nectar
But look! —
I am there, already, at journey's end,

(even as I speak).

I have redeemed the ashes to the wind:
Two diametric loves lie seductively
Before me, on indigo water —

Surely, a tension?

(The Di-Hiraeth)

Truth presses me to my knees,
My lips are puckered to lace the tension
Between.

(I am the love I seek from these ashes)

We shall break our solitude in silence —

(a door shuts behind us)

I am free.

(2/10/98 Regents Park, London)

---

* Safari ya pili: Swahili for 'second journey'.

Phoenix Is Back In Town

Let's take your faith
With us, my fellow dreamer.

Let it
Light our faces.

I must shine at all costs – they expect me to,
Though I died at their own hands.

They squandered my faith
With the impudence of offal seekers.

Only a stranger's faith
Will defy them, my fellow dreamer.

And the stranger's voice
Must be the one to announce
My return: "Phoenix is back in town!"
You must say that twice.

They will run to you, fellow dreamer,
They will mistake you, purposely, for me;
They will see my aura in your eyes
And prefer it to me.
They will praise you for my deeds
Name their walls with your face,
And thank you secretly for mastering my myth so well.

We shall then
Sneak into the wilderness, celluloid forest even,
And change places
For your own return.

(February 1999 Regents Park, London)

for Ifor Thomas

The Street Dancer

Nii Abele Zanzama,
music's only true witness,
makes his way to the next party
to do his thing. He's not expected.

He has forsaken the music kiosk
on the street corner, where he wakes the spirit of song
with his bristling jig and dares
the funk to age him.

And it's not for money. Perhaps gin.

(do we really know him,
or believe the story that he
once taught ballet at La Scala?)

He approaches the rim of sound warily
like a lion cub at a fanged feast.

His bright rags embrace his horned shoulders tightly,
to give new life to his raked smile:

This is a middle-class affair with little space for
spontaneity, let alone drunken street dancers.

But he knows there is always that out-of-place soul
who craves a lull in the affluent tension,
or a final destruction of the myth of
European education — so he waits.

Soon enough that person shouts:

"Have you come to dance for us, Abele?"

All faces turn to him. He beams in the shadows, idling now like a truck engine.

Three or four people laugh —
the signal.

He crosses into the eye of the sound and lets rip.

(20/1/02 Regents Park, London, 3.08 am)

Moondress

The moon wakes her fickle heart –
She follows its single ray
To her favourite bar stool.

The shutters are down,
Only the embers
And an alcoholic dog remain –
The night is not long dead.

If only, she thinks, if only
Her dream husband had come true
And whisked her off this insane stool
that fumes with sin —
Stains of dark rapture.

She grabs the neck of a bottle
Which dances with aphrodisiac roots
And a lingering of corn whisky.
She gulps.

Her solitude stinks.
She used to be the only green tree
In this desert, till self-doubt
Looted the sands from her roots —
Her pride hurts.

She rises furiously from the wiggling stool;
She releases her clothes to the dew outside,
And catches a moondress, on her way
To the solitary oil lamp in the distance.

"This is the last night of avoidance,"
She murmurs, "love can't be that bad."

She is on fire.
The stray dogs cower into the shadows.
She knows a longing oil lamp
When she sees one.
So she races towards
The ancient rendezvous
She set with him
But forgot –
Hope abets her.

Then suddenly the oil lamp dies in the wind;

A scream rings through her veins,
She claws at the bushes
For his shoulders.

He finds her first;
The alcohol leaves her mind.

(27/11/98 Regents Park, London)

Yesu, Yesu
(or song of apostolic imposters)

Witching hour:

Prayerful monsters,
Witches and obeah dealers,
Mingling...mingling

Lightfooted alpha,
exorcist.
The genuflected coin,
Yellow dust, fireflies,
Tambourines, congas
Sand devils, River Jordan,
Rough crossings, rickety crutches,
The deliverance, bandages,
White dove, olive branches,
Bitter, bitter herbs, alabaster wings.

The money music
Mammon is the devil
The music of money

Slashes of fever, Holy water
Slashes of hunger,
Chastity is here:
Sing along now —

Abonsan jee emling
Abonsan jee emling
Abonsan jee emling
Aladura!
Aladura!

Tongues of prophets,
The second coming.

I am the comforter
No Allahu akbar here

King of kings
Nuntsor dientse!

Jerusalem mashi, emashi kpeng.

Giddy trances
The sermon is a zoetrope

Eye of the covenant
Aladura!
Eye of the covenant
Aladura!

Bile
Bile
Bile

Get up and walk, my child!

(Summer 1994, Grangetown, Cardiff)

for Peter Finch

The Beseecher
(or Ode to Avant Garde)

    "Wow!" says he,
With candid disgust fuming behind his voice.

    If released, this whimper
    Would decry you further:

"Who is this crimper of words (our words)
That puzzles even succubus with his scented full-stops;
Full-stops weighted with a secret pain, like veal -
And, when parried, even, becomes ecstatic
Like the rare frisson of a Dinka woman's fingers
Kneading your ego in the dark at Malakal?"*

    O, he is incensed now. He speaks flames:

"And all that mythology of his-
Where has his psyche watered, to roll
With such fuming moss? -
Why can't we find that oasis, too?
... If we try hard enough?"

    What prayer the quartered one holds for you!

"Perhaps, dissect his brain? and play
An alabaster song of it".

    O, what prayer!

"Wherefore," he asks,

    (here he must outdo you with lilting classicism, you see)

"...Wherefore such density
In this breezy ephemeron of time,
Place and name, and scent even?
Wherefore?"

To this baiting enquiry,
You, sage, are advised to be mum.

He is a wily fencer:
Very aquiline behind the tarnished rapier –
His heart festers from the continual
Defeats he suffers in slavish homage
To his 'old masters'.

He has been quartered from light for too long;
His cravings are thus for plain messages only:
Flattery to the dependent mind.

Beware, sage, beware; he is a eunuch,
Unassailable even by the allure of Venus,
Let alone you with but a befuddling wisdom.

He bears you a vengeful gift, quite unlike
Asp venom, but worse still: a racy poison
Unspringable by the lightning zip of love.

(2/10/98 Regents Park, London)

---

*Malakal: an old marketplace in Juba, Southern Sudan, before the Civil War.

for Suzy Sureck

Teardrop - Aqua Lumina

Swift allure
Cleft
Underfoot - lacuna

Horned by thirsty hoofs

The human voices rasp
Between the donkeys' brayings
(swallows in a thorned thicket)
Forlorn in the wake of hope

Once your trickle
Induced infants to wee
The minute before night

Ascetics brand
Their foreheads
In your mirror
Before
Casting your quiet arm
On our lax fontanelles

You

Life's only irony:
Flower of deserts
Teardrop of our God
Vortex of mirages

Sacrament
Sacrament
Sacrament

The voices
You hear
Come from within
You:

"Aqua, aqua, aqua - interdictus!"

They rasp, and sometimes bray
For your mossed faucet
        yet
Like lotus-eaters
– abreast the fuming wall –
we tumble and fight
...and die in your sight

Sing once more
Sing sing like a lambent saffron

(9/8/95 Grangetown, Cardiff, 12.55am)

Vignettes

[1] MEERO

You always break out of the morass
To rediscover sound;
It in hand, you trespass
The chains and the zero.

[2] VISTA

Flagships and tugs, and the
Effervescent yachts
Sail by on desert sands.

[3] MUTE NOTE

The zebu, all Dinka by
Lineage,
Rest their dewlaps
On your anvil - did love
Ever quench your distrust so well?

[4] HOE

Preserve your tooth
In oil:
The labourer needs his mutation,
Like breath.

(2/6/99 Regents Park, London)

Shola The Unknown

Why the stillness? -
First, I mistook you for a supervisor
Sent to knot my flailing tongue,

Then you were betrayed by the slew of
Folders curling in supermarket bags,
Still waiting to be filed away, since the night
Your heart left you and took your mind with it.

I dare say, you haven't lost it all yet,
Keep faith; there's still some hope yet:
That scarf-hooded stare of yours is still working,
Don't you see? even the guard can't stop you
From entering, though he knows you wander.

     But why the stillness? -
     Haven't you heard, dear one?
     No one listens to the meek here.
Or does your pride
     Impede your chaos from flowering.
     We need some chaos, dear one;
     We need chaos to cut chaos, sometimes.

I should know, Shola:
I nearly entered your world once, Shola;
And liberating though it smelt, I bolted;
For fear of stillness.

What brought you this far?
Did you forget not to mix the waters of two great rivers,
And turned into a tree?
Did you mix love with hate, or give hate for hate?
Did you betray yourself to cold curiosity?
Did you test the heavens above?

Or were you betrayed?

Was it on a rainy afternoon like this one?
Did he elope with the snake in high heels?

Or were you sacked from this very office,
     For your pride?
Was it on a dreaded autumn's day like this one, just
When you aimed to crest the sunshine of motherland
With jewels for your beloved mother?

You pace this hall of voices and languid tannoys
Like a ghost.

Once in a short while you look at me, my wife, my son,
With unglancing eyes, as though you rebuke our fall.
We appreciate that. You give us hope.

       In turn we wish to know this:
Where do you sleep and eat? Do you sleep at all?
Do you have any children? Where are they now?
Did you lose an only child?
Did you fail to feed your mother before her death?
Did your children desert you?

Or were you disowned by motherland?

Or are you the mythical Shola of the Diaspora,
Watching silently over your children,
As they grope the ark of mammon
For wild manna?
Do you trust your presence that much?
Will they come to thank you?
Are you waiting for them?

Don't.

They have mistaken their identities for gods.
They hold a mirror to history, and sleep.

Go home, Shola, go home.
Sit near mother's old hearth, with an axe for sureness,
And pour an intoxicating measure for your tired soul;

Denude yourself and
lie on a bed of marble, and cry for yourself,
So as to receive the blessings built on your anguish.

Go home, Shola, you are unknown here.
Go home, Shola, you are wasting here.

But cry to your ancestry to send the chariot,
And let me, your fellow unknown,
Bring your mind from this silence.

(5/10/98 Regents Park, London)

for my siblings, 'Sister' (R.I.P), Enoch and Aferi

ACCORDION BOY

I remember you, Adade!
Is that your name?

I remember your ambling
Into the infernal welcome
Of our courtyard with your
Giant burgundy accordion racing
With brass rivets and tassels - and
A sonorous:

When I Survey the Wondrous Cross

And your proud blind father, whose
Shaky left hand you rested on your elbow,
While you, little prodigy,
Elevated his basso with your soprano,
And massaged the tantalising bellows –

We were mostly a tribe of goose-pimples
While your repertoire lasted:
The subtle clash of his *kong-ka* and your
Accordion was the detail I pursued most
With my inner eye.

I remember how,
long before you reached us,
Akweteyman swayed in the Sunday lull
To your plaintive breeze,
As you guided your small cavalcade
From house to house, rationing
Hymnal levity for resounding alms,

Delivered with those motherly praises, angled
Like parables, to make us,
Your less resourceful peers,
Feel dim with guilt.

They didn't matter a bit to us, and all those
Sidelong after-church looks of damnation our
Grandmothers served us —
You were our own hero.

We envied and admired your virtuosity.

We respected your Biblical obedience to your father;
For we knew we couldn't hack it that well,
Even if paid to.

Most of all, we wished that,
While you sent them into evangelical trance,
Our pious mothers would see the sense
In buying us that Russian flamenco guitar
Gleaming in the *Kingsway* window.

(8/10/98 Regents Park, London)

THE LAST DRUNKARD

You will watch my passage,
I dare you.
You will feed my anguish
With your heart.
I will control your gentility
With my tottering gait.

I have chosen you.

I will make you vulnerable,
I will be a threat to your doorway
And your sublime moments.
I will fall in with your enemies —
They will believe my passion,
For they need my venom.

I have chosen you.

I will drag your rib cage
Into my fetor.
I will slaver at your wife's behind
And say *hoo-ha*!
I will distress your children.
I will soil their bed linen.
I will fall against your wet paint.

I have chosen you.

I will sing when you sleep.
I will urinate in your bathtub.
I will borrow and stain your tie.
I will be sick on your Persian rug.
I will, I will, I will.

I have chosen you.

If all fails,
I will say to you, righteous one,
I will say you are perverted.
I will call you a thief.
I will reign in your name.

I have chosen you.

I am the best.
I am insane, I am the best,
I am crying for help, listen to me.
I need help.

I have chosen you.

(February 1999 Regents Park)

The Inglorious Dying

April:
He saluted the flag,
Then the sun faced away from him
Like his old name —

But he loved the loneliness
And the self-love.

The sucked conscience
That sweeps him away
Each time the dogs howl
At him...

The affinity with washed glass
That denies progeny and faith.

The occasional sycophancy.

May:
A slender song warmed him up:
It was nectar
Sung by the god-servant
At his feet.

He withdrew his sticky fingers
From his abused spout
And licked the aborted swarm.

He gladly consented to fate
And propped himself in bed
To welcome the finite veil.

June:
He hurriedly swallowed all
His gold ingots with water,
His tongue bled.

His eyelids froze.

Then he remembered the tithe
He'd promised his weary servant,
His very own escort out of here —
he panicked about hell.

But a pernicious hand gagged
The swansong in him:

"Too late, sucker,"
Said his god-servant,
"Too late".

(4th March 1997, 4.07pm, Grangetown)

for the pessimist

STONE

You unturned stone,
I will wait for you near my faith,
armed for doubt's sake
with a silver coin,
to panic your lock.

You suitor of anvils
I will wait like a lustful stag,
armed with a full heart
lest your coldness
waylay my innocence.

You stone of dead stones,
I will tease your mesmer's nipples
till you wake, confused,
burning with a phrase for a poem

– Then this poem will be yours to give.

(10/12/01 Regents Park, London, 12.25 am)

for Brendan

PASTORALE

Nightingale,
Gainful acrobat of time,
Playing your poem
On my window pane
At the stab of dawn,

Do you wish to enter?

Will you trust my giving fingertips,
And roll out your tongue
For my dire caress?

Or does the scarecrow below call you
To savour it's numbing terror?

I will protect you!

I'll sweeten the raindrops for you,
And play you jazz,
And preen with you
Like fellow children of God.

(12/6/99 Regents Park, London, 3.30 am)

THE DAY BEFORE

Love lay between their fates
Like a borderline:

(Every border-guard
Craves the otherside).

Roomless,
They stroll the fired grass;
He is a stranger in her town.

They greet the roosting birds,
With their nocturnal hope —

They crawl in the footsteps of shadows,
Begging the sun to blink,
Extending their foodless picnic,
Furtively
Stroking the cusps of their longing,

Their tongues aching
To display their wisdoms, to
Ache each other's heart.

In this cramped energy,
Only their eyes are totally free
To destroy doubt.

Then, at last, the sun curtsies
abruptly like defeat -
>They hear their souls purring in
>the dark;
>They entwine urgently
>Like fighting eels,

(The *Nyayo* police are quiet today)

They fume
In the grass like hatching eggs,
Till the stars tremble
        Into their bodies, and heal them.

    Silence.

They unfold, slowly,
Weeping —

    They would not meet again.

(20/6/99 Regents Park, London, 11.25pm)

Family Home

We left you standing.

Our echoes left
perhaps sooner than us,
through your eaves
like lizards —
virile agama
hoping to signpost time
with a spawn.

You have a crack
right through
the room I shared
with Obuabasah
(his psychedelic graffiti are gone);
a speechless clamour roams
it now: anthill.

Your walls bear
the ashen crust of waste.
Day-old chickens do not
jostle for the heaters anymore,
though I smile hard at the memory –
their barn now harbours
a woman frazzled by life but
intent on hygiene;

I like her astuteness of faith,
but hate her presence
in our space, silent space,
gone space.

(8/2/02 Regents Park, London, 1.30am)

for Maya Angelou

Yet

Poet, let the water run under your feet.
We are your witnesses —
We are riding your shoulders
into the dawn.

We shall see the florist abandon her crust
to lay your watery path with roses;

fireflies haloing your calves will lead a concert
of believers through your footprints

(which will lie resolute thereafter
as if cast in the salt of the Sahel,
for posterity to march through again and again).

Poet, let the water run under your feet.
We are sailing with you
into the better dawn;

where songbirds roost, above history.

(2/4/02 Regents Park, London, 3 am)

for Zynel Bars and Nizamettîn Arîç

THE MYSTERIOUS SONG OF A MODERN KURD

Singing my song on that day of love was something;
if you'd played the oboe to help, I wouldn't have heard it.

And the sun stood squarely above my roof to listen.

> Let's face it,
> it was that kind of rare moment
> when the besieged steal out to play with the wind;

when something in you gives in to an unlived nostalgia,
an imagined memory,

> and you're free to churn the fleeting wind
into accurate statements – lucid non-words – like a miracle maker.

Singing my song on that day of love was something.

> Don't ask me whose wedding it was;
> my brothers and sisters were long scattered
> into the horizon to raise a nation of nostalgiacs,
> detached like lilies on a raft.

I can only say it felt like the wedding of
History and Homeland - quite a couple they made.

> Today, however, I roam these besieged pastures
> like a broken river, rolling and lolling out of shape,
> threshing the rocks for my song,
> to sing again.

(2/4/02 Regents Park, London, 4 am)

ARMAH

Rejected son of Accra,
 your own father hates you like vermin –

>He is ashamed of you –
>He is educated.
>Your mother loves you –
>She has no schooling.
>She travels the land with you
>to distract you, but
>your eyes carry the pain
>like ball and chain.

But you will overcome it –

>You will make a million friends
>and fathers
>to wash away the wicked stain.

You will be a leader and giver.

>Rivers will accept your name
>and you'll have the power
>to cure death.

(23/11/99 Silverlink train - Euston to Watford)

To the beloved memory of Mama

CICATRIX

You are gone now
but left this jewelled scent.
In it I see the past you cleansed of sorrow;
the enchanted sacrifices you lavished
on the six you had left;
the bat you hastened out of the *Enyinam* girders
to free our slumber,
the hymns, the hymns, the hymns,
Jehovah, dignity, kindness, peace,
and your calming stammer
through which you blessed us
even as we fought your
mist alba vigil -

Thus you planted The Deity in us.

Each morning
I bow to this jewelled scent
and thank it for watching over us.

Do you ever hear me where you are?

(12/6/99 Regents Park, London, 3.40 am)

www.ingramcontent.com/pod-product-compliance
Lightning Source LLC
Chambersburg PA
CBHW032102040426
42449CB00007B/1162